My Pet

My Dog

By Sarah Hughes

Welcome Books

Children's Press
A Division of Grolier Publishing
New York / London / Hong Kong / Sydney
Danbury, Connecticut

Photo Credits: Cover and pp. 5, 7, 9, 11, 13, 15, 17, 19, 21 by Maura Boruchow.
Contributing Editor: Jennifer Ceaser
Book Design: Nelson Sa

Visit Children's Press on the Internet at:
http://publishing.grolier.com

Library of Congress Cataloging-in-Publication Data

Hughes, Sarah, 1964-
    My dog / by Sarah Hughes.
      p. cm.—(My pet)
    Includes bibliographical references and index.
    ISBN 0-516-23184-7 (lib. bdg.)—ISBN 0-516-23287-8 (pbk.)
    1. Dogs—Juvenile literature. [1. Dogs. 2. Pets.] I. Title. II. My pet (Children's Press)

 SF426.5 .H84 2000
 636.7'0887—dc21

                                                                00-031633

Contents

Hi, my name is Tommy.

This is my dog.

Her name is Pepper.

5

I take care of Pepper.

I feed her two times a day.

I make sure there is water in her bowl.

7

I give Pepper a bath.

Sometimes she gives
me a bath, too!

9

I take Pepper for walks.

I walk her on a **leash**.

I can take off Pepper's leash at the park.

Pepper finds her friends.

She plays with them.

13

I **trained** Pepper to do many things.

I say, "sit" and Pepper sits.

I say, "shake" and Pepper gives me her paw.

Pepper likes to **fetch**.

I throw the ball.

Pepper goes to get the ball.

Then she will bring the ball back to me.

17

Sometimes Pepper has to see the **veterinarian**.

The veterinarian gives Pepper a **checkup**.

Pepper is healthy!

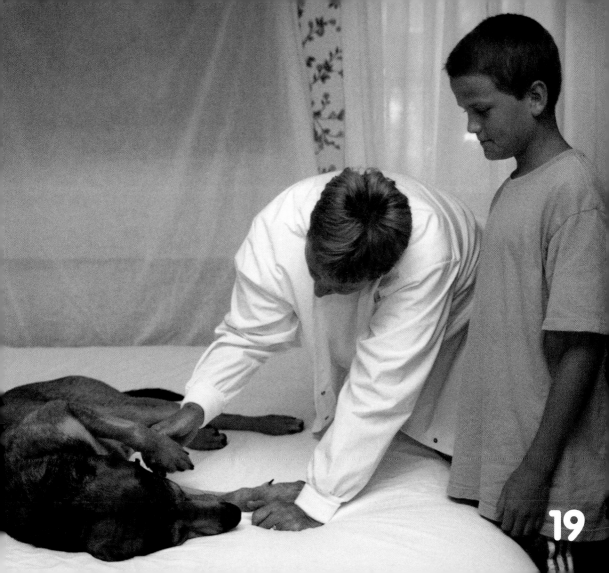

I tell Pepper she is
a good dog.

I pet her all the time.

I love my dog.

New Words

checkup (**chek**-up) a visit in which a veterinarian checks to see if an animal is healthy

fetch (**fetch**) to go get something and bring it back

leash (**leesh**) a long strap used when walking a dog

trained (**traynd**) to teach how to do something

veterinarian (**vet**-uh-ruh-**nayr**-ee-en) an animal doctor

To Find Out More

Books
ABC Dogs
by Kathy Darling
Walker Publishing Company

The Best Thing About a Puppy
by Judy Hindley
Candlewick Press

Web Sites
American Kennel Club for Purebred Dogs
http://www.akc.org
The Kid's Corner includes safety tips and a quiz to help you learn more about dogs. You also can e-mail any questions about dogs and have them answered.

American Veterinary Medical Association
http://www.avma.org/care4pets/avmakids.htm
Find out what you need to do to give your pet the best care.

23

Index

About the Author
Sarah Hughes is from New York City and taught school for twelve years. She is now writing and editing children's books. In her free time she enjoys running and riding her bike.

Reading Consultants
Kris Flynn, Coordinator, Small School District Literacy, The San Diego County Office of Education

Shelly Forys, Certified Reading Recovery Specialist, W.J. Zahnow Elementary School, Waterloo, IL

Peggy McNamara, Professor, Bank Street College of Education, Reading and Literacy Program